PRACTICAL
KNOTS

A STEP BY STEP GUIDE

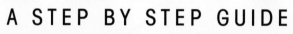

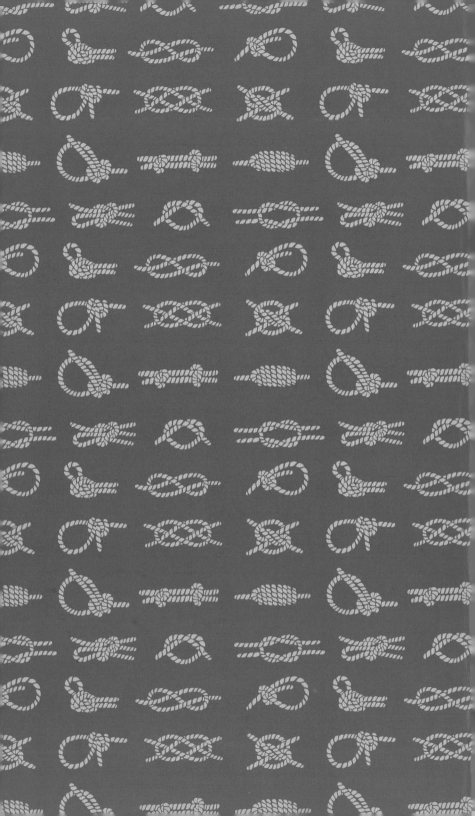

PRACTICAL
KNOTS

A STEP BY STEP GUIDE

BARRY MAULT

ARCTURUS

While all reasonable care has been taken in the preparation of this book the publisher can take no responsibility for the use of the methods described since the circumstances of actual usage of rope and knots are beyond the knowledge or control of the publisher.

If you wish to use rope and knots where there is a risk to life and limb in activities such as climbing, caving, rescue work and the like, you are strongly advised to seek professional instruction beforehand.

Children should always be supervised when learning to tie knots. Never allow a child to place a cord or rope around a part of the body, their own or anyone else's.

ARCTURUS

This edition published in 2017 by Arcturus Publishing Limited
26/27 Bickels Yard, 151–153 Bermondsey Street,
London SE1 3HA

ISBN: 978-1-78404-562-3
AD004459UK

Art Direction: Peter Ridley
Design: Adelle Mahoney
Photography: Bernard Rinaldo
Thanks also to Sarah Blake

Printed in China

CONTENTS

INTRODUCTION

Rudimentary cord made from plant material has been around for more than 30,000 years and, as rope is little use without at least a simple knot, it is safe to assume that knots have also been around for a very long time. The oldest known rope is from Egypt and has been dated to 4,000 years ago. It is likely that this was used on a ship at the time.

Knots are not 'invented', they are discovered and in many cases simply rediscovered, a knot perhaps having been lost as it fell into disuse or was replaced by a gadget of some sort. As anyone who has tried to unravel a tangle of string or wool knows, knots appear like magic all on their own!

So why this book? A knot is only useful if it meets a need and that need may be one normally accommodated by a cable tie (zip tie), Velcro^{tm} or other patent fastening, which is fine as long as you have one handy. However, there are also times when life can be made so much easier or more comfortable with just a piece of cord, a knot and a straightforward guide such as this book.

The development of modern cordage, starting with nylon in the 1950s, has meant that some old seaman's knots may no longer be as reliable as when they were tied in the materials they were designed for, such as manila or hemp. Of course previously unrecorded knots are being discovered all the time.

KNOT NAMES: Unfortunately, in the world of knots, names can be very confusing. Although over time there is acknowledgement that names should change to avoid this confusion – and here the Internet enables such information to be spread very quickly – the fact remains that there are a huge number of books in print with knots shown under a variety of names. Having learned the names of knots over the years, many practitioners are naturally reluctant to change now. In this book, the names used reflect current usage, but a short cross-reference section is included to help with identification. See page 125.

KNOTS IN USE: STRENGTH AND SECURITY: With all knots used for practical purposes you have to take two things into account – knot strength and knot security. These are quite different issues and a basic understanding of each is useful.

KNOT STRENGTH: When a knot is tied into rope, cord or tape, the material, which automatically comes under stress, weakens. How much it weakens is often expressed as a percentage of the strength of the rope, cord or tape before a particular knot was added, but this is at best no more than a rough guide. There are two reasons for this. The first is that there is an assumption that the knot was properly tied and dressed – 'dressed' means that it should be tightened so that it is not distorted in any way. A badly tied knot may substantially weaken the rope over and above the effect a properly tied knot would have had.

The second reason is that laboratory tests of rope (from which the original breaking strength was calculated) were made on new, undamaged rope. The rope being used may have had considerable wear and tear which may not be obvious, so that it already has a lower breaking point which will be further reduced by the addition of a knot.

Fortunately modern synthetic rope has such a high initial strength that, as long as care is taken not to exceed the safe working load (usually about 20 to 25 per cent of the breaking load), there should not be a problem. But if a load is applied suddenly to a rope or cord, e.g. by attaching a heavy weight and dropping it from a height greater than the length of the rope, then the rope or cord may break because the load has not been applied as a steady pull. This is known as shock loading and its effects can be demonstrated by attaching some thin string to, say, two screwdrivers and pulling hard. The string may break under steady pressure, but if the screwdrivers are brought together or pulled apart suddenly the string tends to break more quickly.

KNOT SECURITY: All knots depend on friction. Knot security is resistance to slippage and in practice this is usually far more important than knot strength. Most knots tend to have some initial slip as the knot fully tightens under load and before friction finally takes over, but some combinations of material and knots will slip easily – for example, any ordinary knot tied in fishing line is unlikely to hold, and some knots such as the Granny Knot may slip or jam tightly and become very difficult to undo. Throughout the text, I have tried to indicate whether a knot generally has good security or not, but as conditions of use are not known this cannot always be wholly reliable as a guide.

One of the most important factors in knot security is the proper tightening of a knot (known as 'dressing' the knot). Simply pulling on the end or perhaps the standing parts of a bend rarely works well, leaving the knot prone to distortion and even collapse under load. It only takes a few moments to ensure that all parts of a knot are tightened and all slack removed – the more complex the knot, the more important it is to dress it properly. Please note that, in the instructions for knots which follow, the word 'pole' is often used to refer to any solid upright around which rope or cord is tied.

Barry Mault

Chapter 1

BASIC KNOTS AND ROPEWORK

Preventing a rope or cord from fraying

All rope and cord will fray at the end unless steps are taken to prevent this. The options described below are the quick and simple methods to prevent this happening.

Adhesive Tape

Plastic tape (electrician's or insulation tape) is a quick and easy way to seal the end of a rope or cord. When cutting a piece of rope, put several wraps of tape (about an inch/25 mm along the rope) at the point where you are going to cut it – this will stop both the cut piece and its surrounding area from fraying. Ideally this should be used as a temporary solution, e.g. while tying a plait or complex knot.

Heat Shrink Tubing

Used for electrical wiring, heat shrink tubing usually comes in two forms: with or without adhesive inside (the adhesive version is much more expensive). It will shrink in the heat from a hair dryer (avoid a hot air gun with synthetics as it can melt the rope!). If the tubing is not adhesive-coated, place a piece along the rope and slide well back from the end. Put a small amount of glue on the end 10–15 mm of rope, slide the tubing back over the glue and heat (superglue should not be used – ordinary contact adhesive works better).

Melting the End

Available only for synthetic rope or cord, this is widely recommended for parachute cord (paracord) to seal the ends. Although quick and effective, using a cigarette lighter – the blue part of the flame or the cord will be black from soot – can be dangerous and should never be something children are allowed to do, even under supervision. Always have some water handy since all synthetics will liquefy and burn freely, and droplets of burning material can damage carpets and furnishings. If touched, melting material will stick to the skin and it hurts. The other problem is that, whether this is thin cord or rope, the end can have sharp spikes when cool which can cause injury. Always try and round off the end.

Strangle Knot

A Strangle Knot is neat and effective. Use three or four wraps and pull tight carefully to make sure that all wraps are properly tightened.

Binding the End with Thin Twine (also known as Whipping the End)

This takes time but particularly in heavier rope can be well worth the effort. Two methods are described here: Common or Simple Whipping and West Country Whipping. You will need some thin strong twine (you can buy purpose-made whipping twine which is usually waxed and easy to use).

COMMON WHIPPING

Note: the cord used to illustrate this is much thicker than would normally be used in order to make the illustration clearer.

Lay the end of the twine along the rope with the end of the twine extending well beyond the rope's end. Now wrap the twine tightly about five times around the rope and the twine itself, working towards the end of the rope.

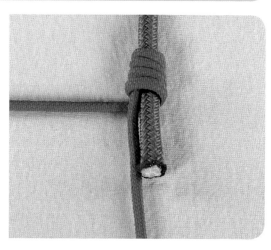

STEP 2

Bring the protruding end of the twine back to form a bight and continue to wrap twine tightly over the legs of this bight, leaving a loop at the end with the end of this loop emerging from under the wraps (see picture).

STEP 3

Tuck the working end of the twine through the loop formed at the end and tug sharply on the end of the loop, which will pull the working end back under its own wraps, trapping it.

STEP 4

Trim off the ends to complete the whipping.

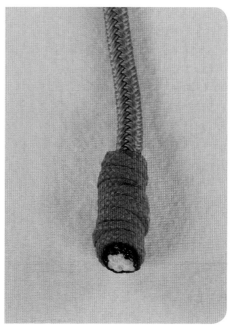

WEST COUNTRY WHIPPING

This is a slightly bulky whipping, but it is quite robust and useful for heavier rope. It is very easy to do and, if it does start to come loose, another Reef Knot can be added at least temporarily. Again, the cord used in the illustration is thicker than that normally used in practice.

STEP 1

Place the centre of the whipping twine beneath the end of the rope and tie an Overhand Knot tightly on top of the rope.

STEP 2

Turn the rope over and tie another Overhand Knot on the back of the rope. Repeat this step until about six to eight wraps have been completed, then add a Reef Knot to each side of the rope.

STEP 3

If the whipping twine was waxed, use a needle to pass the ends through the rope a couple of times to stop them coming undone. If the twine is not waxed, then either pass it through with a needle or add a drop of liquid glue to the Reef Knots to seal them.

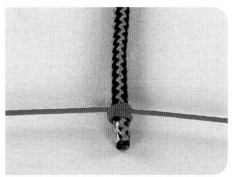

OVERHAND KNOT

The simplest of knots but an effective stopper as it can easily be tightened against something solid with a hole in it. Note that this knot is tied by taking the working end over the standing part – turn the completed knot over and the end now goes under the standing part. As a stopper, either way is equally effective, but occasionally when tying other knots, starting with an Overhand, the orientation may be important.

TO TIE

STEP 1

Take the working end back, over the standing part. Pass the working end up through the loop formed at Step 1, then pull the ends to tighten.

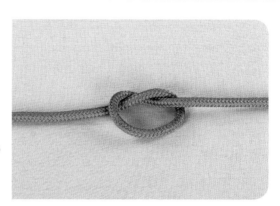

STEP 2

This shows the Overhand Knot from the other side where the working end goes under then over, i.e. the reverse of Step 1.

Uses   This knot will stop thin cord or string from fraying.

FIGURE 8 KNOT

Slightly more bulky than the Overhand Knot and not so easy to draw up against something, but its bulk means it will work where the Overhand is too small.

TO TIE

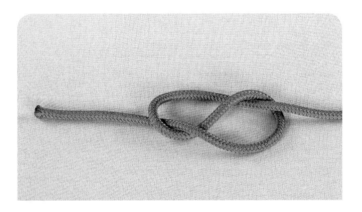

STEP 1

Start as if you are going to tie an Overhand Knot but with the end taken back and over the standing part. Take the end under the standing part and through the original loop.

Uses   A good stopper knot for a rope handle on a bucket or tub or on a swing seat.

ASHLEY'S STOPPER KNOT

Also known as the Oysterman's Stopper, this knot was discovered by Clifford Ashley (author of *The Ashley Book of Knots*) who mistakenly thought he had seen it tied on an oysterman's boat. This is a bulky knot, which can be very difficult to untie once it has been loaded but it is ideal for preventing a rope or cord from passing through a hole.

TO TIE

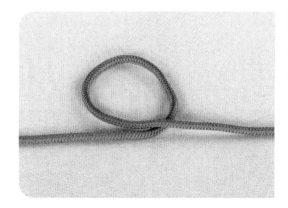

STEP 1

Start with the cord laid out as shown.

STEP 2

Pull a bight of the standing part of the cord up through the loop to form a Slip Knot and tighten the knot around the neck of this loop by pulling on the standing part.

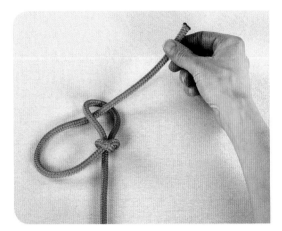

STEP 3

Tuck the working end through the loop from the back as shown.

STEP 4

Tighten the loop to trap the working end.

STEP 5

Pull the working end to finish the knot.

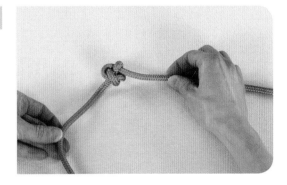

Uses Tie this on the ends of rope going through a swing seat, especially if the holes are large.

Chapter 2
BENDS

Bends are knots for joining two (or sometimes more) ropes together to make one longer rope or to join the two ends of the same rope to make a sling. There are many more bends than are covered in this book, but here you will find a selection covering most if not all occasions when the need arises to join two ropes together.

Unfortunately the language of knots is not always simple: the Fisherman's Bend (or Anchor Bend) is actually a hitch just to confuse the novice (it is said to come from the verb 'to bend', as in to bend a rope to something, i.e. tie a hitch).

Note that where one rope is attached to another other than by intertwining the ends, then the knot used will usually be a hitch (see the Rolling Hitch as an example).

When two ropes to be joined are of different material or different sizes, perhaps stiff or slippery too, then particular care is needed to avoid dangerous slippage. Those which consist of two interlocked Overhand Knots are the most secure (Zeppelin Bend and Hunter's Bend).

Bear in mind when selecting a bend that, whereas some are easy to undo after being heavily loaded, e.g. the Zeppelin Bend, some such as the Fisherman's Knot are almost impossible to untie.

ALBRIGHT KNOT

This is an angling knot used for attaching nylon monofilament to thicker braid, but it is also useful for attaching cord to thick wire. This enables wire to be pulled easily and as an emergency repair. It is simple to tie.

TO TIE

STEP 1

Make a bight in the end of the wire or thicker material (for illustration, rope is used). Lay the working end of the cord alongside the bight and leading back along the standing part of the wire (or, as in this case, rope). Lead the working end back over the bight.

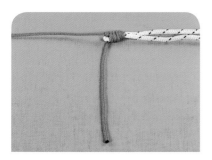

STEP 2

Wrap the cord tightly over the rope or wire toward the bight trapping the cord at the same time – four or five wraps should be ample.

STEP 3

Lead the working end of the cord down through the bight. Slide the knot to the end of the bight and pull on both the standing part and the end to ensure that the wraps are tight.

Uses   Good for joining cord to heavy wire such as fence wire or cordage to heavier rope.

CARRICK BEND

Used aboard sailing ships to join heavy rope hawsers, this is a very secure knot for joining two ropes (and small cordage) and if it has been under load it can still be worked loose to undo it. The first method of tying (also used in tying the Lanyard Knot) takes a little while to learn, but the second method is almost a parlour trick. It is so easy to remember that it makes inclusion of this knot worthwhile.

TO TIE – METHOD 1

STEP 1

Arrange the left-hand (white) rope as shown with the right-hand working end under the standing part. Lay the second (red) rope under the loop of the white rope with the working end to the left.

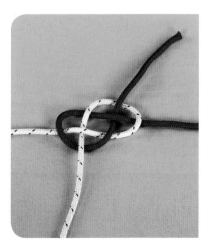

STEP 2

Bring the working end of the left (white) rope to point downwards. Now take the working end of the right-hand (red) rope down across the standing part of the white rope and lead the red rope in an under-over sequence as shown in the picture. The red rope finishes with the working end on top of the loop of the white rope.

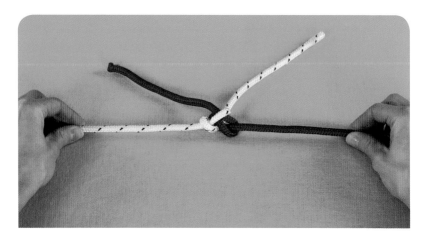

Tighten the knot by pulling on the standing parts then the ends to set it properly. The knot collapses into the compact form shown in the picture with both ends on the same side.

TO TIE – METHOD 2

STEP 4

Make a bight in each rope (or the ends of the same rope) with the working ends on the outside.

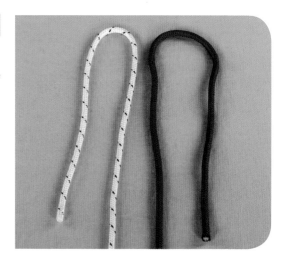

Uses   This is the basis of the Lanyard Knot and well worth learning.

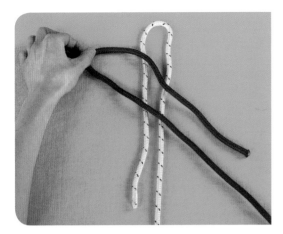

Place one bight over the other making a 'V' formation (it doesn't matter which side goes on top).

STEP 6 Take the working end of the bight on top and lead it under the knot and up through its own bight. Repeat for the working end of the bight underneath, but this time go up and over the knot and down through its own bight. Work some of the slack out of the knot (or the ends will tend to come out of it), then simply pull steadily on the standing parts – the knot will gradually collapse into its final form – tighten as at Step 3 above.

FISHERMAN'S KNOT

The Fisherman's knot is an excellent knot for cord and string. It won't slip and is very strong but for heavy-duty use then the double version is recommended. This knot is used by climbers to make slings and is ideal for making a sling to use with the Prusik Knot. It is, however, almost impossible to undo if it has been loaded, but ideal if the two ropes or cords need to be permanently joined.

TO TIE

STEP 1

Lay the two ends side by side but facing in opposite directions, then take the right-hand working end and tie an Overhand Knot around the left part.

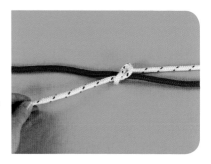

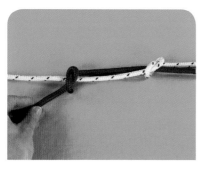

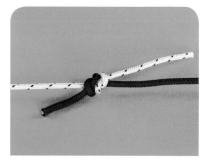

STEP 2

Turn the knot around so the ends face in opposite directions and repeat Step 1 – tie an Overhand Knot again. Tying it this way ensures that when tightened the two Overhand Knots will sit together neatly.

STEP 3

Tighten the Overhand Knots individually, then pull on the standing parts and the overhands will slide together and lock.

TO TIE THE DOUBLE FISHERMAN'S KNOT
Start with Step 1 opposite.

STEP 4

Take the right-hand working end and make a round turn around the left standing part going back over the working end.

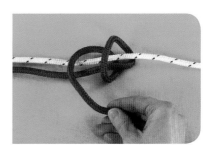

STEP 5

Now tuck the end of the right-hand cord back under the cross made by the turn at Step 2 and tighten. Turn the knot around so that the ends face in opposite directions and repeat Step 2. Tying it this way ensures that, when tightened, the two Strangle Knots will sit together neatly.

STEP 6

Tighten the Strangle Knots individually, then pull on the standing parts and the Overhands will slide together and lock.

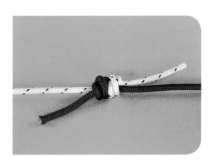

Uses   The double version joins stiff and slippery material such as plastic-coated washing line.

HUNTER'S BEND

This was thought to be a new knot back in 1978 when its supposed discovery by the late Dr Edward Hunter was widely publicized. In fact what Dr Hunter had discovered was a new and simpler way of tying the knot previously published some years before by Phil D. Smith as the Rigger's Bend, but the publicity inspired a small group of enthusiasts to meet and form the International Guild of Knot Tyers in 1982.

Like several knots, it consists of two interlocked Overhand Knots and it's good for joining two ropes or cords, though it may jam under moderate to heavy load and, therefore, be difficult to undo.

TO TIE

STEP 1   Lay the two ends side by side but facing in opposite directions.

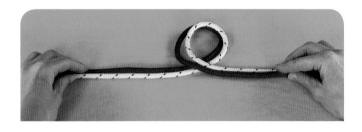

STEP 2

Take hold of both cords to the right of centre and fold them over to the left to form a pair of loops as shown.

Uses   You can join two or more ropes to make a tow rope with this knot.

STEP 3

The loop in the left-hand (white) cord now sits on top and the loop in the right-hand cord (red) sits underneath. Take the end of the upper loop (white) down around the legs of both loops and up through the middle.

STEP 4

Take the end of the bottom loop (the red) and lead it up, around both loop legs again and down through the loop. The red end is now pointing down and the white one is pointing up as they leave the two loops.

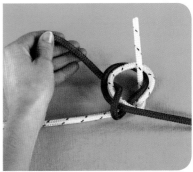

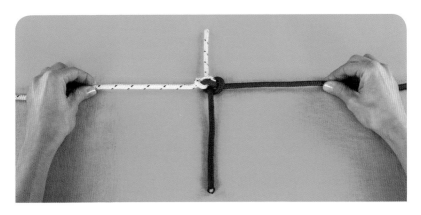

STEP 5

Finish the knot by pulling the standing parts and the ends to work it tight (the ends will stick out at right angles to the joined lines). Note that on each side of the knot there is a bight on top – contrast this with the Zeppelin Bend shown later.

LAPP KNOT

A relative of the Sheet Bend, this knot has long been used by people in the far north (along with the Eskimo Bowline). It is faster to tie than a Sheet Bend and as easy as a slipped knot (perhaps its most common form). Warning: the orientation of the ends in a Sheet Bend is important – in a Lapp Knot it is crucial. If tied incorrectly, it will slip and this can be dangerous, so ensure both ends of the knot lie on the same side.

TO TIE

STEP 1

Take the end of one rope and fold it back to form a bight, with the end away from you.

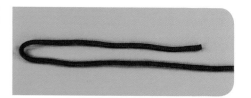

STEP 2

Lead the working end of the second rope away from you, over and round the bight, and tuck the working end over the turn and down through the first rope's bight.

STEP 3

The completed knot is shown slipped, with the working end doubled over as a bight rather than simply tucking in the end.

Uses

Hang items from a backpack by making a sling with the slipped Lapp Knot for instant access.

REEF KNOT (LOCKED)

The Reef or Square Knot is a binding knot and is not recommended as a bend, but it is included here because it can easily be locked to make it secure – though it can be difficult to untie if heavily loaded. If you're used to the Reef Knot, this simple adaptation is easy to remember. Anyone familiar with macramé will recognize this as the start of Solomon Bar, though it is tied in a different way.

TO TIE

STEP 1

Start by tying a loose Reef Knot.

STEP 2

Take each end in turn and tuck it down below the knot, around and up underneath the two parts in the middle. (This is similar to Step 4 of the Becket Hitch.)

STEP 3

Tighten carefully using both the standing parts and the ends.

Uses

A Reef Knot is the one most people remember – this tuck will make it secure as a bend too.

SHEET BEND

The Sheet Bend is a very old sailors' knot, which though an excellent knot in its day may not be so secure in modern stiff and slippery materials (especially climbing tape). It is not usually tied in rope. The double version gives extra security, especially if the ropes to be joined are of different thicknesses. See also the Lapp Knot.

TO TIE THE SHEET BEND

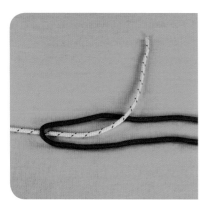

STEP 1

If one rope is thicker, then make a bight in the end of the thicker rope and place the end of the second rope under the bight and over the end of the first rope as shown in the picture. If both ropes are of similar thickness, then it doesn't matter which way round they are used.

STEP 2

Continue with the second rope around the back of the bight in the first and tuck it under itself. Make sure that the ends of both ropes are on the same side of the knot.

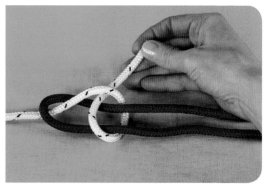

Uses   Fix a broken shoelace with this knot.

DOUBLE SHEET BEND

STEP 3

To make a Double Sheet Bend follow the instructions in Steps 1 and 2 above, but having tucked the working end under itself, take it around the first rope again and tuck it under itself for a second time.

SLIPPED SHEET BEND

The Slipped Sheet is quickly undone (as long as it has not been subjected to a very heavy load) by pulling on the end of the rope or cord which has been tucked as in Step 2. It is ideal as a temporary bend.

STEP 4

Start as at Steps 1 and 2 (and if required, Step 3 as shown), but instead of tucking the end make a bight in the rope and tuck the bight as shown. Pull the end of this bight to undo the knot quickly. A Slipped Sheet Bend is normally tied as the single rather than double version, but this is shown for illustration.

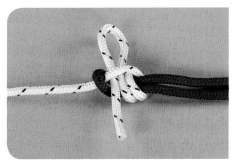

STEP 5

The completed knot.

WATER KNOT

The Water Knot is a bend specially designed for flat material such as a strap or tape (especially climbing tape). It can be tied in rope, but there are better bends available. Easy to tie, it is used to make tape slings as well as joining two tapes.

There is a recent variation on this knot called the Beer Knot (so named because it is said to be an improvement on the Water Knot and beer is better than water!). How to tie this is explained below.

TO TIE

STEP 1   With one tape (or one end), tie a loose Overhand Knot near to the working end.

STEP 2

Now take the other tape end and, working backwards through the first Overhand Knot, trace the patch of the first tape until the working end emerges alongside the standing part of the first tape. Tighten carefully. If this knot is to be used with a heavy load, make sure that the two tail-ends are at least several inches long.

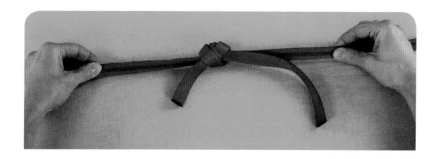

STEP 3

The completed knot.

Uses   Good for joining flat material such as a broken strap.

THE BEER KNOT

This works only with tubular climbing or lifting tape (which is sold and used flat). As the tapes are used with one end inside the other, pictures are not really useful here. The Beer Knot is normally used to make a very secure sling as follows:

STEP 1   Tie a loose Overhand Knot about halfway along the tape.

STEP 2   Insert one end inside the other until they overlap by about 30 cms (12 ins) – this is not easy and you may need a stick (e.g. a garden cane) or piece of stiff wire to push one end inside the other.

STEP 3   Carefully move the loose Overhand Knot until it is about halfway between the overlapped ends. Hold the tapes at both sides of the knot firmly and tighten the knot. Before using this sling always make sure (by touch) that the inner end has not slipped.

ZEPPELIN BEND

This knot gets its name from a story about Charles Rosendahl, a US Navy officer. It's said he insisted on using this knot to tie down his airship back in the 1930s, which sounds like a guarantee of a pretty good knot. It is perfectly likely that the knot was in use before then, but the idea has stuck and the knot is now associated with him and his airship.

The knot is made up of two interlocked Overhand Knots but arranged differently from Hunter's Bend. The method of tying shown is sometimes called the 'b & q' method and this is an easy way to remember the sequence.

It is a very secure knot with the advantage that, even after a very heavy load, it is easy to undo. It can be used to join two ropes of different size and material – even an extreme difference as shown below.

It is widely regarded as one of the best bends available and highly recommended.

TO TIE

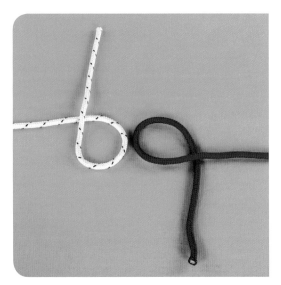

STEP 1

With the left-hand (white) cord form a 'b' with the end lying on top of the standing part and with the right-hand cord form a 'q' with the end lying beneath the standing part.

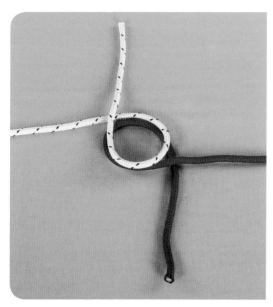

STEP 2

Place the left-hand (white) loop on top of the right-hand (red) loop as shown.

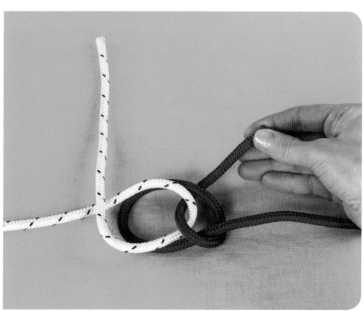

STEP 3

Take the right-hand (red) end (from the 'q') and bring it over the legs of the two loops and down through the middle.

Take the left-hand (white) end (the 'b' end) and take it around the back of the legs of the two loops and up through the middle.

STEP 5

Tighten the ends and standing parts evenly. This is one of very few knots which, if it loosens, can be tightened simply by pulling on the standing parts. Note that in this knot (unlike Hunter's Bend), there is a bight on opposite faces of the knot.

ROPES OF WIDELY DIFFERING DIAMETERS

STEP 6

Make the knot as in Steps 1 to 5, but use the thicker rope to form the left-hand part (letter 'b'). Before tightening the knot, take the right-hand rope working end around the loop of 'b' (the white rope), again following its own path back up through the knot.

STEP 7

Now tighten carefully to form the knot.

Uses   Join two or more ropes to tow a car as this knot is easy to undo after heavy loading.

Chapter 3

HITCHES

Hitches probably offer the greatest variety of practical knots. A hitch is used to attach rope or cord to another object – and possibly another rope.

Some specialized hitches are designed to attach a rope to a pole or another rope where the force applied is along the rope or pole at a very shallow angle. These knots can be moved by holding the knot in hand and sliding it but will grip once in position and the load is applied.

HALF HITCH AND ROUND TURN & TWO HALF HITCHES

A Half Hitch is not usually used alone but is an essential component of other knots – not least the Round Turn & Two Half Hitches (below) and the Buntline Hitch. The structure of a Half Hitch is simple and it is usually tied around its own standing part.

It is ideal either alone or with other knots to ensure that a pipe, tree branch etc. can be pulled in a straight line (see the Timber Hitch for an example).

TO TIE

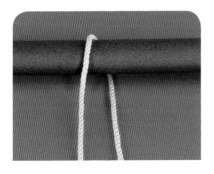

STEP 1

STEP 2

Take the working end of the rope over the object and around to the right of the standing part.

The working end now goes around the standing part, forming the Half Hitch.

ROUND TURN & TWO HALF HITCHES

This is a classic hitch which is strong, secure and reliable as well as easy to remember. The initial round turn means that some of the load is taken up by friction. Loosen the knot slightly and you will see that the working end has made a Clove Hitch around the standing part, but unlike the Buntline Hitch the second Half Hitch will not be trapped against the attachment point, making this hitch a little less secure but a lot easier to undo.

TO TIE

STEP 1

STEP 2

Take a complete turn (known as a round turn) around the rail, or whatever the hitch is to be attached to, leading to the right.

Tie a Half Hitch around the standing part.

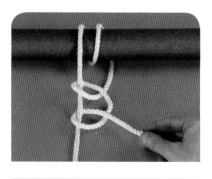

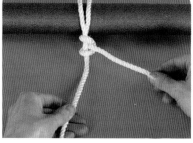

STEP 3

STEP 4

Repeat Step 2, tying a second Half Hitch below the first one. Both Half Hitches should be the same with the working end emerging to the right.

Tighten by first pulling on the working end then the standing part to slide the knot up to the attachment point.

Uses A Round Turn & Two Half Hitches works for anything, from tethering an animal to setting up a washing line.

ANCHOR HITCH

Shown in many books as the 'Fisherman's Bend', this knot is a hitch not a bend which is confusing – the old name probably arises from sailors 'bending a rope' to something. It is more secure than a Round Turn and two Half Hitches and can be used, as the name implies, on a small boat anchor which is out of sight. There are two ways to finish this knot though; some arborists (tree surgeons) who choose to use this as a tie-in knot to a harness, stop at Step 2.

TO TIE

STEP 1

With the working end, make a complete turn around the ring or bar to which the knot is attached.

STEP 2

Take the working end over the standing part and lead it under the turns around the ring or bar. This makes a Half Hitch trapped by these two turns.

STEP 3

Use the working end to make a Half Hitch around the standing part. Tighten and make sure the knot is pressed close to the attachment point.

STEP 4

Alternatively repeat Step 2, i.e. take a second turn under the Round Turns as shown.

Uses   Fasten the fixed end of a rope with this when tying down luggage on a roof rack

BECKET HITCH

The Becket Hitch has essentially the same construction as a Sheet Bend, but rather than join the ends of two ropes or lines, it is used to join a line to a fixed loop (note: it will not work if the loop to which it is being attached is made of something other than cordage or rope, e.g. metal or wood). If the ropes are of different types or size, then the Becket Hitch can be doubled or tied in a different way to provide a more secure attachment.

TO TIE – STANDARD METHOD

STEP 1 Lead the working end up through the loop and around the back of the loop.

STEP 2

Take the working end back over the loop and under itself. If the knot is to be doubled, then repeat this step. A back-up Overhand Knot tied in the working end will add some security against slippage.

TO TIE – SECURE METHOD

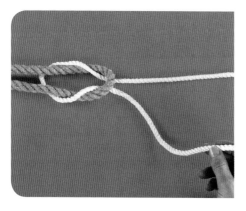

Pass the working end up through the loop, around the back of both loop legs and over and down through the loop again. At this point, the two ropes have the appearance of a Reef Knot.

STEP 4

Lead the working end underneath the standing part and thread under its loop legs. Work tight.

STEP 5

The knot after tightening.

Uses Join a cord to the sling through a tool handle to make a safety lanyard.

BLAKE'S HITCH

Devised by Heinz Prohaska and first published in 1981, this hitch was later popularized by climber Jason Blake, whose name it now carries. Used mainly by arborists, it is a slide-and-grip knot for use with one rope on another. However, as in most if not all slide-and-grip knots, the rope used to make the hitch should be thinner than the main rope. It can, of course, be used to make an adjustable loop such as a guy line.

TO TIE

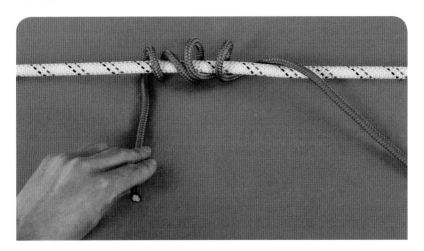

STEP 1   With the working end make four turns around the rope to which the knot is to be attached in the opposite direction to the pull (the first two turns should be kept loose, so tying these around the thumb can be helpful).

Uses   Makes a heavy-duty adjustable loop for a guy line.

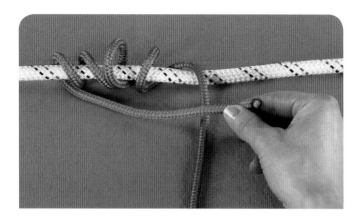

STEP 2 With the working end emerging from behind the rope, bring it down and over the standing part.

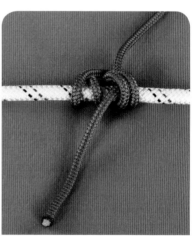

STEP 3 **STEP 4**

Now tuck the working end under the first two turns around the back of the main rope.

Tighten all parts carefully before use. Particularly if this knot is being used in a critical situation, add an Overhand or Figure 8 Knot to the working end to prevent it pulling out if the knot twists.

BUNTLINE HITCH

A very secure hitch which will jam tight if subjected to even a moderate load. It is useful where it will remain in place for some time without needing to be undone. It is very similar to the Round Turn & Two Half Hitches, but the Round Turn is usually omitted.

The Clove Hitch tied around the standing part still consists of two Half Hitches but tied in reverse. The inner Half Hitch is tied second and presses against the attachment point locking it in place. For ease of release, this second Half Hitch can be made with a bight rather than the end, making a slipped Buntline Hitch, but as with all slipped knots a heavy loading may still jam the knot tight.

When tying this knot, it is easy to make a mistake and and tie another similar knot. Instead of tying two Half Hitches in the form of a Clove Hitch, you may find that you have tied a Cow Hitch with the second part on the inside. This knot is called a Lobster Buoy Hitch and is actually less likely to jam tight, so you may want to try this deliberately as an alternative!

TO TIE

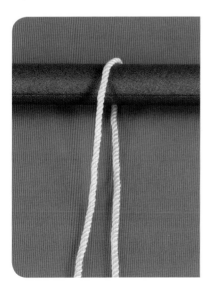

STEP 1

Place the working end over and under the attachment point (which may be a ring or rail for example) rather than a Round Turn.

Uses   Use this to attach the line to the metal ends of a suspended clothes airer.

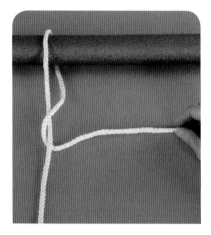 

STEP 2

Lead the working end over the standing part to the left and under to the right.

STEP 3

The working end now goes up towards the rail (or whatever) and over and under the standing part to form a second Half Hitch between the first Half Hitch and the attachment point.

STEP 4

Tighten the knot and slide up to the attachment point.

CLOVE HITCH

The Clove Hitch is another very old knot used at sea. It is what is known as a 'mid-line' knot, meaning that it is designed to be used to attach the middle of a rope to another rope or post (or whatever), once the ends have been securely fastened. An example would be a series of stakes which need to be held in a line: here, a Clove Hitch is used round each stake, except the first and last, where a more secure end-of-line hitch would be needed (e.g. the Gnat Hitch or two Half Hitches). It is, however, most commonly used to attach a rope end to a post or rail, even though it can either jam tight under a heavy load or – especially if it is allowed to rotate – come adrift. So if you are using it as an end of line attachment, exercise caution.

TO TIE AROUND A RAIL

STEP 1

The working end goes over and under the rail to the right and then over the standing part to the left.

STEP 2

Now take the working end over the rail again and lead it back under the rail and underneath itself. The standing part and working end will lie side by side in parallel but point in opposite directions.

TO TIE IN HAND

This method works where the completed knot can be dropped over the end of a post – it cannot be used around a railing, for example, if the ends of the railing cannot be accessed.

STEP 1

Make an Overhand Loop in the rope as shown.

STEP 2

Now make a second loop in the same way as the first.

STEP 3

Place the second loop behind the first loop and the knot is ready to be placed over a post.

Uses Link a series of canes or temporary fencing with Clove Hitches which are easily adjusted.

COW HITCH AND GIRTH HITCH

The Cow Hitch (which gets its name from its use for tethering animals) is an excellent hitch as long as both ends are loaded – otherwise it will slip, but it can be locked with a simple tuck which makes it secure, in which case one end should be left relatively short.

TO TIE WHERE ONLY ONE ROPE END IS AVAILABLE

STEP 1

STEP 2

Lay the working end over the rail, rod or pole to which the line is to be attached.

Take the working end around to the left, back over the standing part and under the rail to the right.

STEP 3

Bring the working end forward over the rail and down under itself to complete the knot. This completes the Cow Hitch.

TO TIE WHERE BOTH ROPE ENDS ARE AVAILABLE

Make a bight in the rope, place the bight over a rail or through a ring and tuck both ends through this bight. Pull both ends to tighten.

If the rope is a sling (a closed loop), then the same procedure is used with the main part of the sling replacing the two ends (as in two interlocked rubber bands). In this configuration the knot is known as a Girth Hitch.

Uses The Locked Cow Hitch can be used to anchor the end of a Trucker's Hitch.

TO LOCK THE COW HITCH

STEP 4

Start with a Cow Hitch, with one end quite short.

STEP 5

Lead the short end behind the long end, over the top of the bight (through which the ends go), passing under both of the parts encircling the rail or ring to which the knot is attached. Work tight.

DRAW HITCH

The Draw Hitch is a 'fast getaway' hitch. It is a secure fastening to a rail, yet with a sharp tug on the working end of the rope it comes completely adrift instantly. This hitch is secure under load and is to be preferred to the better-known 'Highwayman's Hitch' which is not as secure. Use it in any case where a quick release may be required, especially in an emergency.

TO TIE

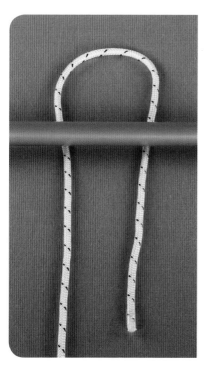

STEP 1

Make a bight in the rope and, with the end to the right, place the bight behind the rail to which it is to be attached.

Uses Hang tools and other items from a rail for instant access.

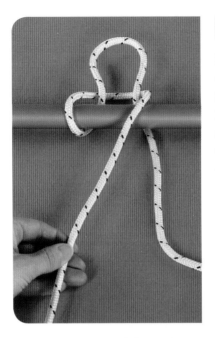

Lead the standing part
of the rope over and
behind this first bight.
Bring the standing part
down in front of the rail
to the left of the rope
working end.

Finally make another
bight in the end of the
rope and pass this
bight through the first
bight from the front of
the rail, passing over
the standing part.
The completed knot
is shown loose for
clarity and needs to
be properly drawn
up before any load
is applied. To release
the knot, pull on the
working end sharply
and it will come away
cleanly.

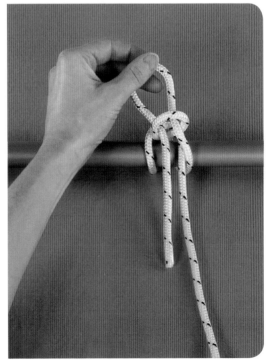

GNAT HITCH

The Gnat Hitch is a recently published knot on notableknotindex.webs.com. A hitch designed to act like a noose when attaching to a bar or ring with only a single pass round with the rope, it is jam-resistant unless subjected to a very high load. Easy and quick to tie as well as being secure, this little hitch is well worth learning.

TO TIE

STEP 1	Lead the rope over the attachment point and tie a Half Hitch around the standing part as shown.

STEP 2	Lead the working end to the left behind the standing part.

Now tuck the working end down through the loop to the left of the standing part.

STEP 4 Tighten the knot, then pull on the standing part to slide the knot up against the attachment point.

    The completed knot is small and neat.

Uses Useful in the garden for attaching string to garden canes or hanging a bird feeder from a branch.

GROUND LINE HITCH

This is a neat and simple little hitch for attaching a rope to a rail, pole or another rope at right angles. Commercial fishermen use it to attach nets and crab and lobster pots to the main rope. As a hitch for attaching the end of a rope, it is superior to the Clove Hitch – it is more secure and will not jam. Do not attach it to a post which does not have a round cross-section. It will not hold properly to a square post. There is an almost identical hitch – the Picket Line Hitch. This hitch is tied from right to left, whereas the Picket Line Hitch is tied from left to right. Use whichever method of tying is the easiest to remember.

TO TIE

STEP 1

Take the working end to the right around the rail or rope to which it is to be attached.

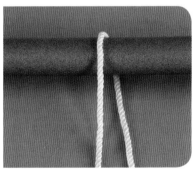

STEP 2

Lead the working end to the left over the standing part, around the rail etc., and back over itself. Tuck the working end under the standing part and tighten.

Uses   A good knot for hanging boat fenders. In the garden, it ties a line to a garden cane (or the first and last in a series).

KNUTE HITCH

Named by the American master rigger Brion Toss, this simple hitch is probably quite old. It is used to attach a cord to a tool or anything with a hole in the handle. Attached in seconds and released as quickly, this is a very handy way to hang something, as well as to provide a lanyard attachment, especially if working at height.

TO TIE

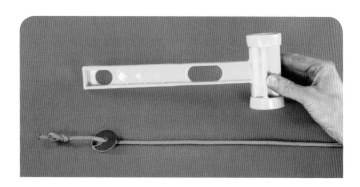

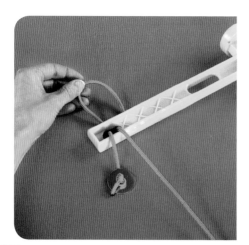

STEP 1

Tie a Figure 8 Knot in the end of a piece of cord. The doubled cord must be able to fit through the hole in the handle but if the hole is big, place a washer on the cord end before tying the Figure 8. The illustrations show a washer being used because the hole is too big.

STEP 2

Make a bight below the Figure 8 Knot and push the bight through the hole in the handle.

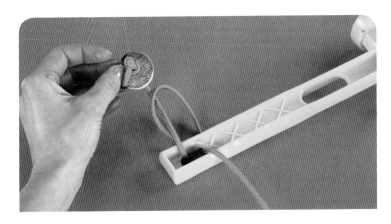

STEP 3

Bring the Figure 8 Knot (and washer if used) either around the side of the handle or over the top and through the protruding bight.

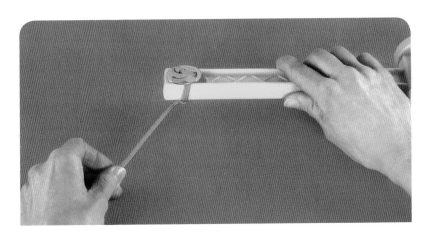

Uses Use to attach rope to the eyelets of a tarpaulin for easy removal without undoing any knots.

STEP 4

Pull tight. To remove the cord, loosen the knot and push the Figure 8 back through the bight.

MARLINSPIKE HITCH

The Marlinspike Hitch is used to quickly attach a bar (such as a marlinspike or a screwdriver) to a cord or rope to provide a handle to pull. Although nothing more than a simple noose, it is very handy when, for example, a Constrictor or Strangle Knot needs to be pulled very tight. Simply place a Marlinspike Hitch on each end of the binding cord and heave.

TO TIE
The tying method reflects the way the hitch is used.

STEP 1   Form an Overhand Loop in the cord.

Uses   Use with a spanner or similar to give purchase when trying to drag something heavy such as a log.

| STEP 2 | Holding the loop at the point where the rope crosses itself fold the loop to the left over the left-hand standing part. |

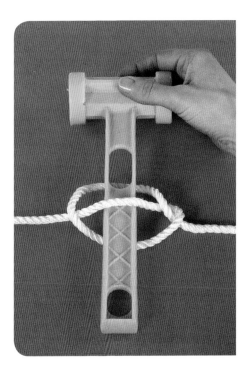

STEP 3

Insert the bar, screwdriver etc. (in this case a hammer handle) underneath the centre part going over both sides of the loop. Pull in the direction of the Overhand Knot – in this example, this will be to the right.

PILE HITCH AND DOUBLE PILE HITCH

A hitch which is very easy to tie and yet has very good security. This can be used as a mooring hitch, tied in the middle of a line to place rope between stakes and tied around a bar such as a spanner to provide a handle to haul on a line, e.g. when tying a Strangle Knot or Constrictor (see also the Marlinspike Hitch). The Pile Hitch is not recommended where the end of whatever it is being attached to is not available (for example, a floor-to-ceiling pole). There are easier hitches to tie in these circumstances.

The Double Pile Hitch gives extra security if the line is slippery.

TO TIE

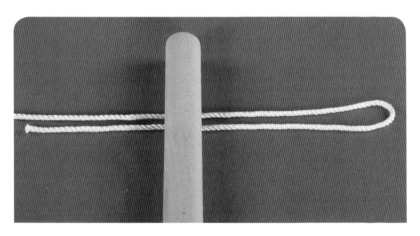

STEP 1 Make a bight in the rope and place it alongside the post etc.

Uses If used for a temporary mooring, e.g. on a canal with a bank stick, it is easily cast on and off.

| **STEP 2** | Wrap the bight around the post or rail spiralling away from the end of the post or bar. |

STEP 3

Now lift the end loop and lift it over the wraps and then over the end of the post. Tighten the knot.

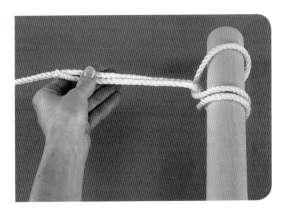

TO TIE A DOUBLE PILE HITCH

STEP 4

After Step 2 above, wrap the bight around the post once more and repeat Step 3 above. Tighten the knot.

PIPE HITCH

The Pipe Hitch is used to pull or lift a cylindrical pole, e.g. scaffolding. It can also be used to attach a rope to a pole where the pull is along the length of the pole. There are many knots which will do this job, but the Pipe Hitch is very simple and easy to remember as well as being effective.

TO TIE

STEP 1

With the working end of the rope make several tight wraps around the pole away from the direction of pull. The number of wraps depends on how slippery the pole is and how heavy it is. An absolute minimum of four wraps is recommended.

STEP 2

Take the working end back to the standing part and tie two Half Hitches around the standing part at the point where the first wrap starts. And that is all there is to it.

Always test before raising or lowering a heavy pole and add more wraps as necessary.

Uses Hang garden tools with a smooth handle such as a hoe or rake.

PRUSIK KNOT

Devised by Dr Karl Prusik from Austria, this knot has become a classic slide-and-grip knot for use on rope. Unusually, it will grip in either direction. It is always made using a sling, either one made of rope (in which case the sling should be of thinner rope than that to which it is being attached) or one specially made and available from outdoor/climbing suppliers (though these are relatively expensive and not designed for everyday use).

As well as its common use in climbing, it is useful in any circumstances where a 'rope handle' needs to be attached to another vertical rope, e.g. to hang a hook with a tool bag. It can also be used as part of the Trucker's Hitch, in which case a relatively short sling will take the majority of the wear and is easily replaced.

TO TIE

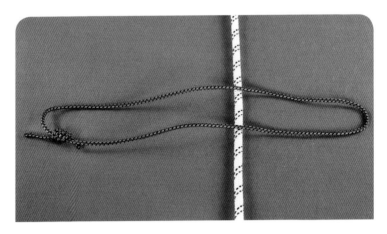

Uses On a vertical pole such as scaffolding, it holds a hook for a paint tin or a bucket.

STEP 1

Place a bight of the sling across the main rope.

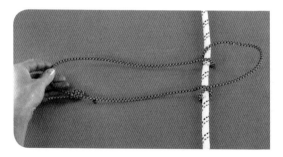

Lead the bight under the main rope and tuck the remainder of the sling down through this bight.

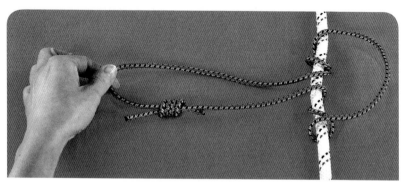

STEP 3

Now take the bight down under the main rope and around again in the centre between the first wraps. Again tuck the remainder of the sling down through the bight. (If the rope is icy or slippery, a third turn can be taken, making a Double Prusik.)

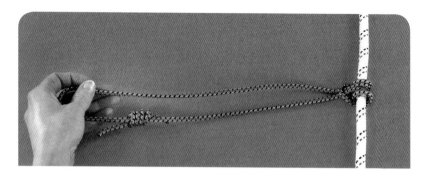

STEP 4

Work the coils tight, making sure that they are parallel and not crossed – the main loop of the sling must emerge from the middle of the wraps.

ROLLING HITCH AND TAUTLINE HITCH

The Rolling Hitch can be used to attach a rope to a smooth pole, e.g. scaffolding, where the load will be along the pole or other solid rail. In this configuration, it is a Clove Hitch with at least one extra turn. It can also be used to attach one rope to another – possibly as a means of joining a thin rope to a much thicker one (arguably, it is then being used as a bend), when the method of tying is similar but slightly different. This is handy when only a short line is available to tie another rope to, say, a boat painter. The Tautline Hitch is the name for a Rolling Hitch used to make an adjustable loop at the end of a rope – for a guy line perhaps. All versions of this can be slid by hand to adjust the position of the attaching rope, but will grip under load. See also Blake's Hitch, Pipe Hitch, Prusik Hitch.

TO TIE THE ROLLING HITCH TO A SOLID POLE

STEP 1 **STEP 2**

With the working end make at least two complete wraps around the pole in the direction of the pull. On a slippery surface and/or with slick rope add more turns.

Take the working end back over the pole and the wraps and tie a Half Hitch to the left of the standing part. Work tight before loading.

TO TIE THE ROLLING HITCH TO A ROPE

STEP 3

As with a solid pole, use the working end to make at least two wraps but this time trapping the standing part as shown and working away from the direction of pull.

STEP 4

With the working end tie a Half Hitch around the pole.

STEP 5

Work the knot tight by pulling on both the working end and the standing parts.

The Tautline Hitch uses this same method, but the working end is taken back to the standing part to form a loop.

Uses   Use a Rolling Hitch to attach a line to a short painter rope when towing a dinghy.

TENSIONLESS HITCH

This seems to be a misnomer as a rope attached using the hitch is of course under tension. The name, however, refers to the residual tension after the end of the knot which, because of friction, is not bearing any load.

The Tensionless Hitch is an anchor knot used in rescue situations but is also very useful for more mundane tasks such as hanging a swing – especially a monkey swing or car tyre from the branch of a tree or a swing frame. It is very simple to tie but does need the addition of a large (depending on rope diameter) shackle or a carabiner.

TO TIE

STEP 1 Make a small loop (an eye) in the working end of the rope – a Figure 8 Loop or an Angler's Loop is recommended.

With the working end, make several wraps around the tree limb or whatever – how many will depend on the strain on the rope and how rough or smooth the tree limb is, but a minimum of three wraps and as many as five may be needed. Once wrapped around the tree limb, pulling the standing part should not cause the wraps to slip (so add more as needed).

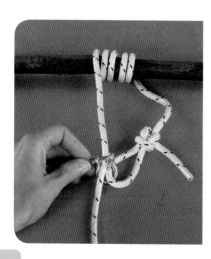

STEP 3

Attach the shackle to the eye of the working end and around the main standing part. This will stop the rope from becoming unwound, e.g. in a high wind.

Uses Ideal for attaching garden or tree swings.

TIMBER HITCH

This is more accurately a noose but is invariably used as a hitch which is quickly and easily made and just as easily undone; it cannot jam. Its name comes from its being used for pulling large logs as it can easily be released and retied. Being remarkably secure, it is a handy noose for many applications. It is often used to start a rope lashing. See the example overleaf showing how to hang heavy-headed tools in a shed or garage.

When a Half Hitch is added (which enables a log or pole to be pulled lengthways), the combination is known as a Killick Hitch.

TO TIE

STEP 1

Lead the working end around the log, then over the standing part and under the loop just formed.

STEP 2

Now wrap the working end around the leg of the loop, so that the standing part runs through a small eye, making a noose. Be careful to wrap around the loop leg, which was made by the working end. If using laid rope, make the wraps in the same direction as the lay of the rope (if done correctly the rope will fit neatly in the lay).

When the standing part is pulled, the noose will tighten and the wraps will be trapped against the log.

Following these steps without tying it round anything will produce a free-standing noose.

ADDING A HALF HITCH

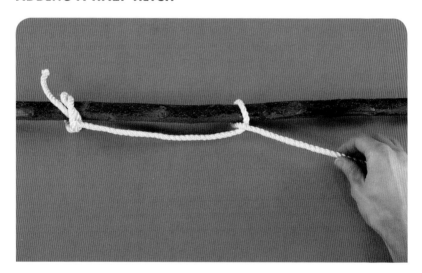

STEP 4 Take the standing part of the rope toward the end of the log in the direction in which it is to be pulled and place a Half Hitch around the log itself. Adjust the Half Hitch, so that when the standing part is pulled, the Half Hitch grips the log near to the end but not too close (in case it slips off).

EXAMPLE USE FOR LIFTING TOOLS – IN THIS CASE A HEAVY HAMMER

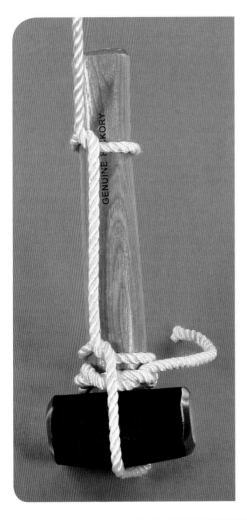

STEP 5

Make a Timber Hitch around the shaft of the hammer close to the head of the tool. Lead the standing part of the rope over the head and make a Half Hitch over the shaft of the hammer close to the head. Now make a second Half Hitch around the shaft nearer to the end of the shaft.

This will enable the hammer (or pickaxe, sledgehammer etc.) to be raised with the heavy head pointing downwards, avoiding it tipping over and causing injury (which can easily happen if it is hung head upwards by a loop around the shaft). The rope is easily removed. If the item is likely to stay in place for some time or is being raised, or lowered, from height, a fixed loop may be substituted for the Timber Hitch.

Uses   Attach to a tree branch and lead the rope over a higher branch to keep control when pruning. Add a Half Hitch to drag cut branches.

Chapter 4

LOOP KNOTS AND NOOSES

This chapter covers loops of a fixed size and nooses which are loops where the size of the loop is adjustable. Slings, loops formed by joining the two ends of a rope, are also included, though the knots for joining the ends are invariably bends. Nooses are sometimes referred to as slip knots, but please note that a slipped knot – one which can be undone by pulling the end – is quite different and examples will be found amongst the bends, e.g. the Slipped Lapp Knot.

OVERHAND LOOP

A simple but secure loop which is very difficult to undo once it has been loaded. Useful in string rather than rope because it does jam tightly, this can also be tied near to the end of the line to form a stopper knot.

TO TIE

STEP 1

Make a bight in the end of the line and, using the bight, tie an Overhand Knot in the doubled line, so that the bight emerges to form a loop at the end.

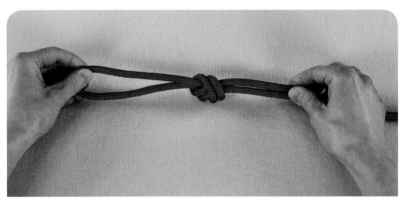

STEP 2

Tighten by pulling the loop away from the standing part and working end.

Uses   For hanging anything with a hole in the handle either on its own or in combination with a Girth Hitch.

FIGURE 8 LOOP

The Figure 8 Loop is tied the same way as the Figure 8 Knot but using a doubled rope – Step 3 shows the knot loosely tied for comparison.

TO TIE

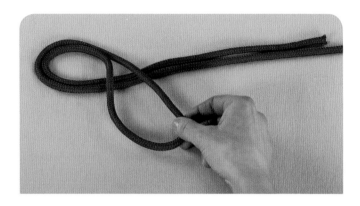

Start as if you are going to tie an Overhand Knot using a doubled rope taking the single loop over the standing part again.

STEP 1

STEP 2

The single loop goes under the standing part and through the loop formed by the doubled rope. It is tied in the same way as a single line Figure 8 Knot but using the doubled line.

ALTERNATIVE METHOD OF TYING

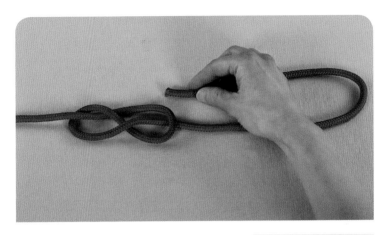

This shows an alternative way of tying the loop by starting with a simple Figure 8 Knot and with the working end retracing the knot to form the loop (this method is used by climbers to attach a rope to their harness). Be careful to keep the two parts parallel as you retrace the knot.

STEP 3

Uses A strong loop which works well in the end of stiff material – attach a vehicle tow rope to a ring or bar by the retracing method.

ANGLER'S LOOP (ALSO KNOWN AS THE PERFECTION LOOP)

An old fishing knot used originally in gut but still useful in modern synthetic line. Prone to jam in cordage or rope if subjected to a heavy load, it is nonetheless a very secure knot ideal for string or cord when untying may not be needed. Works well in elasticated cord where most loop knots do not.

There are two methods of tying this loop. The first is very easy if what is needed is a loop in the end of a cord, whereas the second method can be used to make the loop around an object or through a ring.

METHOD 1

STEP 1

Make a bight in the rope with the working end to the left. Take the working end under and over the standing part to form the main loop to the right. It is this loop, which determines the size of the final loop of the knot.

STEP 2

Take the working end and wrap it around the standing part.

Uses   Will make a secure loop in elasticated cord for use on a trailer with fixing hooks on the side.

METHOD 2

STEP 3

Pick up the main loop and lead it through the initial bight in the standing part. Pull tight.

STEP 4

Make a simple Overhand Knot in the rope at the point where the loop knot is needed, but note that this knot is formed by going under then over.

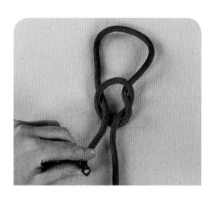

STEP 5

Take the working end of the rope around (or through) the object to which the loop is to be attached and back through the loop of the Overhand Knot (this makes a slip knot).

STEP 6

Lead the working end underneath the standing part and back under the top of the Overhand Knot and underneath itself. This will be clear from the picture. Tighten carefully and the knot will be similar to that in Step 3.

BOWLINE

Pronounced 'bo-lin' this is known as the 'king of knots', not least because it has been used at sea for hundreds of years. The name comes from the bow line attached to the edge of a sail. It is simple to tie, won't jam and is always easy to untie, though as with most knots, not while it is under load. To distinguish the basic knot from variations, it is referred to as the 'Common Bowline'.

The knot has two drawbacks. When not under load, it can loosen if it is jostled or shaken – this is known as 'slack security'. With slick artificial fibre rope which may be stiff and springy, the Bowline can be more prone to loosening, though it is still safe under load for everyday use. The second problem is known as 'ring loading'. This is where the loop is stretched wide which may cause the knot to collapse. For more secure versions, the Double Bowline, the Water Bowline and Scott's Lock for the Bowline are good alternatives.

For a double loop version of the Bowline, the Bowline on a Bight is very useful, not least because if both of the standing parts are loaded, the knot cannot come undone accidentally. It can be tied without using the ends.

TO TIE

STEP 1

Make a small Overhand Loop (a nipping loop) with the working end of the rope.

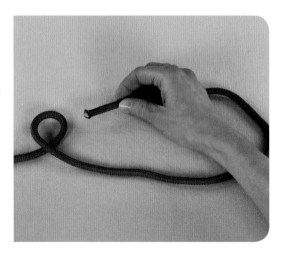

STEP 2

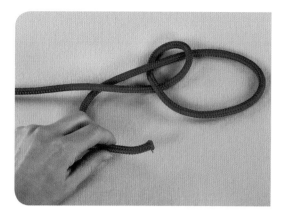

Take the working end up through the small loop formed at Step 1 and around the back of the standing part. Note that the small loop is on the right and the working end goes to the left.

STEP 3

Bring the working end back down through the small loop, following the same path as before.

Tighten the knot carefully and note that the end is inside the loop.

SCOTT'S LOCK

This was devised by Scott Safir, an American member of the International Guild of Knot Tyers. It is a simple addition to the Common Bowline but one which adds considerable security and is very effective at preventing the knot from working loose when not loaded.

Bowline Uses

General purpose loop afloat and ashore. The loop to use if ease of untying is important.

Scott's Lock Uses

Climbers' harness tie-in and good mooring loop as it it is unlikely to loosen in blustery conditions.

TO TIE

STEP 1

First tie a Bowline but leave the knot loose. Now you are going to take the working end over the rim of the nipping loop and down through it. In the picture a white rope is used to illustrate the path of the end which is shown completed at the next step.

STEP 2

This is the completed knot (loose).

STEP 3

First tighten the original Bowline, then pull on the working end to complete the dressing of the knot.

BOWLINE ON A BIGHT

This knot has two loops which are independent. If both standing parts are loaded, this is a closed system which will not slip. Ideal for use where two separate anchor points are required or where a line has to be split into two at an attachment point, not least because this knot can be tied without using the ends of the rope.

However this method is no use if the double loops have to pass through a ring or similar, but the knot can be tied to a harness, for example, by starting with a Common Bowline and retracing the knot with the working end.

TO TIE WITHOUT USING THE ENDS

STEP 1

Make a long bight in the rope and, using the doubled rope, make an Overhand Loop as if starting a Bowline with the doubled rope. Bring the end loop up through this Overhand Loop.

Uses   Enables a load to be split across two anchor points for safety.

Now take the end loop, open it up and take it completely over the knot. Continue to take the end loop back up behind the doubled standing parts.

STEP 3

To tighten take hold of the two strands which are the continuation of the loop now sitting around the standing parts and pull them out to form a double loop. Be careful not to make a slip loop by pulling out the wrong part. Once tightened, this is a secure double loop.

TO TIE USING ONE END

STEP 4

Start by tying a loose Common Bowline, but make sure that the working end is much longer than usual. Take the working end parallel to the leg of the loop next to it and follow this around the original knot.

STEP 5

Continue following the knot round until the working end emerges alongside the standing part.

DOUBLE BOWLINE

The Double Bowline (also called the Round Turn Bowline) is somewhat more secure than the Common Bowline and very easy to tie. It has a double nipping loop which affords more grip in stiff or slippery material.

TO TIE

STEP 1   Start by making two Overhand Loops, one on top of the other (this is different from the Water Bowline where one loop is placed underneath the other).

Uses   Provides a little more security, often used on a mooring rope.

As with the Common Bowline, take the working
end up through the loops made at Step 1, around
the back of the standing part and back down
through the two nipping loops, ending up inside
the main loop.

STEP 2

Tighten carefully – note that one of the nipping
loops is tightened by pulling on the main loop leg.

STEP 3

WATER BOWLINE

The Water Bowline is so called because after immersion in water (where vegetable fibre rope will swell) it is still easy to undo. It offers more security than the Common Bowline.

TO TIE

STEP 1

Make two Overhand Loops and slide the second loop under the first to form a Clove Hitch. This variation is sometimes known as a Clove Hitch Bowline.

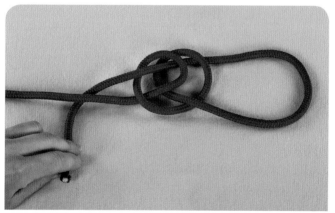

Follow the same procedure as Step 2 for the Bowline, but pass the working end up through both loops, and around the back of the standing part.

STEP 2

| **STEP 3** | Bring the working end back down again through both loops. |

| **STEP 4** | Carefully tighten the knot. Note that under load the two loops of the Clove Hitch may separate, but this is to be expected and does not mean that the knot is slipping. |

Uses   More secure version of the Bowline...

BOWSTRING KNOT

The Bowstring Knot is one of the simplest and also one of the oldest knots known. It is found all over the world. As an adjustable loop, it has limited use because of the limited range of adjustment, but it is so quick and simple to tie as well as being surprisingly secure that it deserves to be better known. It is unusual in that other nooses will tighten when the standing part is pulled, but the Bowstring Knot loop gets bigger, so it can be used as a temporary dog collar and lead without risking choking the animal.

The Bowstring Knot has one additional feature. The loop it makes is, if kept fairly small, almost perfectly round. For this reason, it is the basis of the Honda Knot (from the Spanish word 'honda' meaning a sling), the knot used to make a lariat. The round loop allows free movement of the lariat noose so that it does not harm an animal.

TO TIE

STEP 1

Tie an Overhand Knot in the rope far enough from the end to allow for the desired loop size and pull the working end down.

Uses   Good knot for a guy
line on a tent etc.

STEP 2

Take the working end up and around the back of the Overhand Knot and up through the eye formed in the Overhand Knot. It is essential that the knot is tied exactly this way – if the end is tucked through the Overhand Knot any other way it will slip.

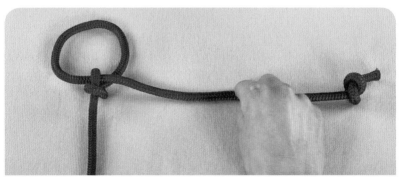

STEP 3 Tighten the Overhand Knot to trap the working end which will form a loop. This loop can be adjusted easily by pulling on the working end or by pulling the working end back out of the Overhand Knot. Surprisingly, the working end does not slip (at least not easily) if the loop is loaded, but an Overhand Knot in the end will prevent it from slipping out completely.

The Honda Knot has an Overhand Knot added to the working end up against the point where it leave the Overhand Knot, making it a fixed and round loop into which a rawhide, metal or plastic liner (called a 'burner') is added to prevent wear on the loop.

BUTTERFLY LOOP

Sometimes referred to as the Alpine Butterfly (it was published in *The Alpine Journal* in the 1920s), it is a very secure and strong loop tied in the middle of a rope – the ends of the rope are not used. This knot will take a load in any direction.

Apart from its value as a loop, it can also be used to isolate a section of damaged rope. The knot can easily be tied around the hand and the size adjusted as it is tied.

TO TIE

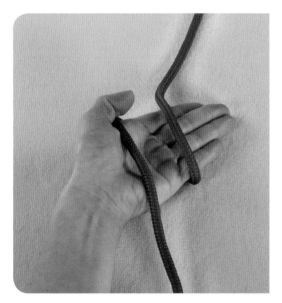

STEP 1

Make two turns around the hand.

Uses   Isolate a section of damaged rope with this loop. Useful as part of a Trucker's Hitch.

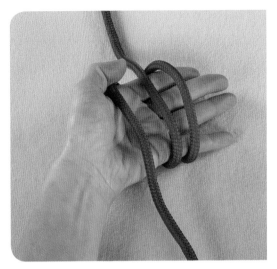

STEP 2

Take the rope around again, but this time between the first two turns.

STEP 3

Lift up the bight to the right and take it to the left over the other two turns. If a section of rope is damaged, then the damaged part should be within this turn.

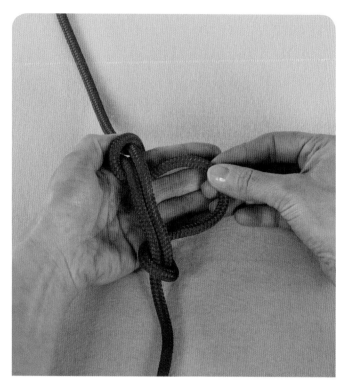

STEP 4

Now continue with the bight at Step 2 and lead it to the right underneath the two turns.

STEP 5

Remove the knot from your hand and tighten carefully, starting with the loop at the top. The completed loop is at right angles to the main line.

ESKIMO BOWLINE

This variation of a Bowline was in use by Inuit people long before being discovered by the Arctic explorer Sir John Ross in the 19th century. It has greater resistance to ring-loading than an ordinary Bowline – that is, if the loop is pulled outwards, widening it rather than in line with the standing part, it will not collapse. It is also easy to make this into a slipped loop, as shown, so that it can be undone rapidly.

TO TIE

STEP 1

Make a nipping loop in the line as if starting a Common Bowline.

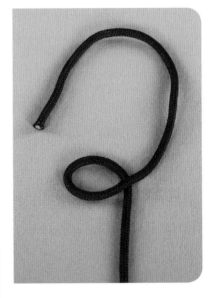

STEP 2

Take the working end down through the nipping loop (the opposite way to the Common Bowline).

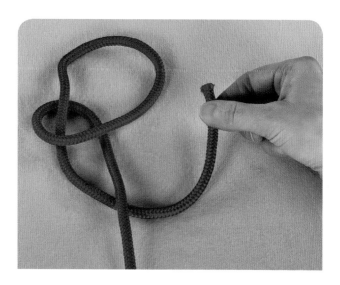

Lead the working end under the opposite side of the standing part and back over.

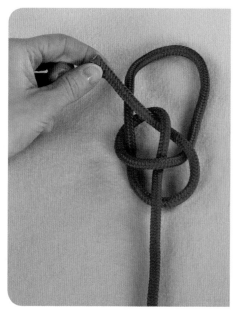

STEP 4

Now take the working end back parallel to its original path through the small nipping loop first formed.

STEP 5

Tighten carefully and check that one face of the knot has the three-part formation shown in the picture.

SLIPPED KNOT VARIATION

STEP 6

At Step 4 opposite, make a bight with the working end and tuck this bight as shown in the picture.

Uses   Moor to a large bollard with this rather than the ordinary Bowline.

FARMER'S LOOP

Another midline loop which is very easy and very quick to tie around the hand. It is strong and secure too.

TO TIE

STEP 1

Wrap the rope around your hand twice so that there are three cord parts side by side.

STEP 2

Lift the middle cord and move it over to the right.

STEP 3

Now lift the new middle cord over to the left.

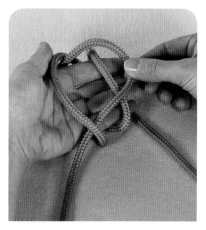

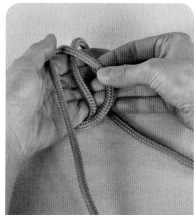

STEP 4

Lift the new middle cord again to the right.

STEP 5

Holding the middle cord, lift it up and remove the cord from your hand, pulling this loop and tightening the knot below it.

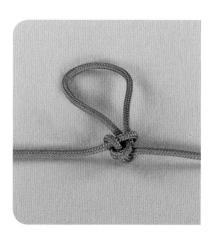

STEP 6

This is the completed loop.
    Remember this sequence as:
middle to right
middle to left
middle to right
middle goes up.

Uses   Useful for the
          Trucker's Hitch rope
          pulley mechanism.

POACHER'S NOOSE

This is a noose knot which tightens as load is placed on the standing part and grips well, though it will collapse completely unless there is something in the loop to stop it, such as a thimble to prevent the rope from chafing – especially with material such as plastic-coated washing line which is soft and easily abraded.

It also makes a good noose hitch for attaching a rope to a shackle or similar hardware. It will work in elasticated cord, but take care that the hardware to which it is attached cannot be forced back through the knot if the cord stretches.

TO TIE

STEP 1

Make a bight using the working end, then taking the working end, wrap it twice around the standing part and itself, working back toward the loop. A third turn can be added for extra security if required (when technically the knot becomes a Scaffold Knot).

Uses   Place a section of tarpaulin over a smooth pebble, tighten a Poacher's Noose around the neck trapping the stone and you don't need an eyelet.

STEP 2

Lead the working end back through both turns (three if used) made at Step 1 and tighten the knot. Reduce the loop to the size required by pulling the standing part while sliding the knot toward the loop.

STEP 3

If a thimble is to be used, insert it into the loop before finally tightening. Work the thimble into place as you tighten the knot since it will have a tendency to slide round out of position.

LANYARD KNOT

This is a classic and good-looking loop knot used when making a lanyard for anything from a knife to a name badge. Until recently, it was regarded as more decorative than practical, but the development of new and expensive synthetic materials has led to the use of the Lanyard Knot for items such as soft shackles, since other knots will slip in these immensely strong but slippery materials which have little or no stretch.

Nevertheless, for everyday materials, this is a handsome little knot which is easy to tie.

TO TIE

STEP 1

Start by joining the ends of a single cord by weaving a Carrick Bend but leave it flat as shown. This can be done by the two overlaid bights method, but you need to be careful to ensure that the standing parts are pulled only until the knot can be flattened to the form shown in the picture. Placing the knot over your hand tends to be easier.

STEP 2

Take the left-hand end down to the right (in the same direction that it is pointing in), over the leg of the loop and up through the centre of the Carrick Bend.

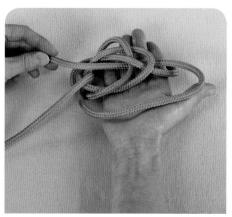

STEP 3

Now take the right-hand end up to the left, over the leg of the loop and up through the centre of the Carrick Bend alongside the left end (both should be pointing in the same direction, away from the main loop).

STEP 4

Hold the two ends in one hand and the loop in the other hand and gently work the knot together. The knot may not tighten properly by simply pulling unless the cord is fairly slippery, so work the parts of the knot tight carefully.

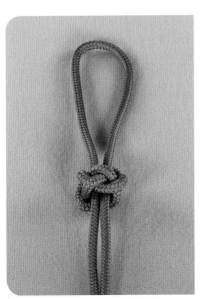

STEP 5

The finished knot fully tightened.

Uses   In thin cord it makes a simple zip pull. Soft shackles often use this knot.

Chapter 5
BINDING KNOTS

Binders are knots used to tie around one or more objects to form a firm wrapping. This may be anything from a bundle of sticks to a parcel, from a roll of carpet to a chair frame being glued together.

CONSTRICTOR KNOT

The Constrictor Knot is a binding knot which needs a convex surface to bear down on, but is ideal for at least temporarily sealing a rope end or to tie around any bundle to hold it firm without slipping or even, in an emergency, to hold a hosepipe to a tap or metal pipe.

There are two tying methods. The first is used where it is convenient (or necessary) to tie the knot around something; perhaps the object is large or the end impossible to reach. The second method is tied 'in the bight', which means that it is tied in hand and then placed over an object. This makes sealing a rope end much easier, for example, but it does take a little practice to get the action right.

Warning: no matter how it's been tied, a Constrictor Knot is very difficult to undo once it's been tightened and, like the Strangle Knot, it should never be tied around a part of the body.

TO TIE DIRECTLY AROUND SOMETHING

STEP 1

STEP 2

Take the working end of your cord to the right over the object, or bundle to be bound, around the back and over itself to the left finishing at the back of the rope or cord.

Lead the working end up and over the standing end and beneath the crossed cords on top of the object. This forms an Overhand Knot trapped underneath the wrapping cord.

STEP 3

Pull both ends hard to tighten. See the Pile Hitch and Marlinspike Hitch on pages 60 and 62 for knots which can be used to attach the ends of the Constrictor to two screwdrivers or spanners to provide handles with which to exert a very heavy pull on the ends (but be careful not to damage whatever this knot is tied around).

TO TIE IN HAND

STEP 4

Start by folding the cord in an Underhand Loop as shown.

STEP 5

Bring the rear part of the loop down over the standing part.

STEP 6

Twist the lower loop to the right to form a Figure 8.

STEP 7

Now fold the lower part of the figure under and upwards so that you now have two loops, one on top of the other.

STEP 8

This is now a Constrictor Knot, so place the two loops over whatever is to be bound and pull the ends to tighten.

Uses A damaged hosepipe can be temporarily repaired with Constrictors holding the ends of the hose over a short piece of rigid pipe.

GLEIPNIR

This knot was discovered in 2009 when it was posted on the forum of the International Guild of Knot Tyers by Anthony Dahm using the pseudonym 'Gleipnir', hence the name used for the knot. (The word 'Gleipnir' is from Norse mythology and refers to the binding that once held the mighty wolf Fenrir!)

The knot itself is very simple but ingenious. It forms a binding around just about anything with the distinct advantage that, unlike the Constrictor and Strangle Knots, it does not need a convex surface to bear down on. It is sometimes called a 'mid-air binder'.

The detail of tying shown below is for a slight variation to the original knot but uses the same principle. You will need a cord long enough to pass around the bound object twice, with enough left over to complete the knot.

TO TIE

STEP 1

Double the cord and, with a finger in the bight, twist once.

STEP 2

Fold the small loop formed in the twisted cord back on itself and, holding this loop, place the doubled cord around the object to be bound.

STEP 3

Take one end of the cord and feed it over and back through the loop at the end. Feed the other end straight through the loop, so that the two ends now point away from each other.

STEP 4

Pull the two ends in opposite directions to tighten the loop and lock the binding in place. If this is to be left unattended, each end can be half-hitched around the doubled cord to secure the knot (though this may prove difficult to undo later).

TO UNDO THE KNOT

Identify the end which passes straight through the nipping loop (not the end which was brought over and through) and pull on the standing part below the knot to pull this end back through the knot. This will cause the whole structure to loosen. If Half Hitches were added, then these must be undone first.

Uses   Holds the legs of a chair or stool firmly while waiting for glue to set.

POLE LASHING

The Pole Lashing is a handy way of tying a bundle of sticks, canes or poles together which is easy to undo later. It can also be used to sling a plank by arranging the knot slightly differently.

TO TIE

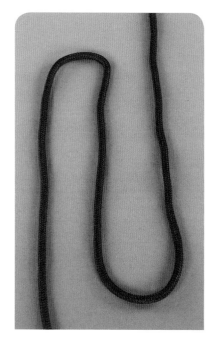

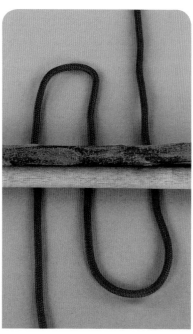

STEP 1

Arrange the cord in a 'Z' shape, as shown.

STEP 2

Place the poles over the cord leaving a bight and one end at the top and at the bottom.

STEP 3

Place each end through the bight on the opposite side of the bundle and work the slack out of the knot.

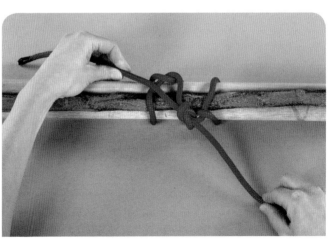

STEP 4

Tie the ends in a Reef Knot on top.

TO SLING A PLANK OR SIMILAR

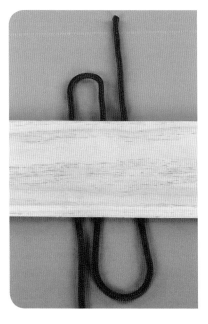

STEP 5

Start as at Steps 1 and 2 on page 110.

STEP 6

Instead of working out the slack to bring the bights together, arrange one bight on each side of the plank. The rope ends can be knotted together to hang the plank or perhaps a shelf.

STEP 7

To sling a plank on edge bring the bights to the top as shown.

Uses Two of these knots – one at each end – will support a suspended shelf.

REEF KNOT

The Reef Knot is a binding knot (its name comes from its use in reefing sails – tying around a sail once it has been 'reefed' or taken in). It is widely used as a bend but should never be used to join ropes where the material or size of the ropes is different OR there is a risk of injury if it comes undone.

It has the advantage (and disadvantage) that it is easily undone by a sharp pull on one end which collapses the knot. However, it lies flat once tied (hence its once common use in bandages) and holds well if it is binding a roll of material, perhaps cloth.

The tying steps below are often remembered thus: 'Left over right and under, right over left and under', but this can be reversed to 'Right over left then left over right' if preferred.

TO TIE

STEP 1

Take the left-hand working end over and under the right-hand working end.

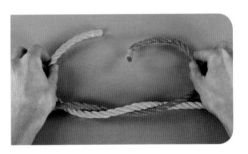

STEP 2

Now take the working end on the right over and under the (now) left-hand working end. The ends are now back on the same sides that they started out and the knot is neat and symmetrical.

Uses An emergency first aid sling or a bandage is finished with a Reef Knot – it lies flat and is easily untied.

STRANGLE KNOT

The Strangle Knot is a binding knot which needs a convex surface to bear down on, so among other things it is ideal for putting a temporary binding (whipping) on the end of a rope to stop fraying. Once tightened, it is at best very difficult to undo and may need to be cut off for removal. Unlike the similar Constrictor Knot, the ends emerge from the sides of the knot rather than the middle, so it looks neater, especially when tied with multiple wraps.

Warning: never tie a Strangle Knot around any part of the body.

Tip: when tying this knot, especially with multiple wraps, use a piece of bent wire under the wraps to make it easier to pull the end back through.

TO TIE

STEP 1

Take the working end over to the left and under the rope to which it is being tied (or bundle etc. as appropriate) at least once but as many times as required (more than four wraps is difficult to tighten though), bringing the end back over the standing end.

| STEP 2 | With the working end, make an Overhand Knot by taking the working end over and under the standing end. Lead the working end under the wraps to the right (see picture). |

| STEP 3 | Pull hard on both working end and standing end to tighten. |

Uses   Quickly stops the end of a natural fibre rope from fraying.

Chapter 6
MISCELLANEOUS KNOTS

These are either knots which do not fit easily into a category, such as the Cat's Paw, or are a combination of knots used together to make up a whole such as the Trucker's Hitch and the Versatackle.

They are included because they are practical even if they are only known about by a few people.

CAT'S PAW

This knot is used when a rope is taken over a hook, so that if the load becomes unbalanced it will not immediately slip to one side. Once removed from the hook, it falls apart instantly so it cannot jam.

TO TIE

STEP 1

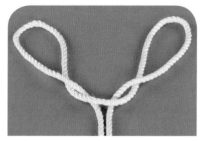

Make a bight at the centre of the rope and turn the bight back over the standing parts, forming two loops.

STEP 2

Twist each of the loops two to three times in opposite directions (placing a finger into each loop is an easy way). The left-hand loop twists clockwise and the right-hand loop anti-clockwise. Add more twists if the load is very heavy.

STEP 3

Bring the two loops together and place over the hook – make sure that the number of twists on each side is the same. Pull on both standing parts to tighten the knot around the hook.

Uses   When hanging wide items from a wall hook or nail on a single cord, this stops the item from sliding sideways.

TRUCKER'S HITCH

The Trucker's Hitch is the classic lorry driver's method of tying down a load. Tied originally with vegetable-fibre rope such as hemp or manila, it amplifies the force used to heave down a rope over a load. The original method which uses a nipping loop like a Bowline is not easy for the occasional user, so here are three safer and easier methods. The basic design is the same no matter how it is tied, so the instructions below can be adapted in several ways. The steps below show the structure rather than the knot in use.

TO TIE

Anchor one end of the rope to a fixed point on the truck on the opposite side to where the rope is to be tied off. A slipped Buntline Hitch is common as is a Round Turn & Two Half Hitches or an Anchor Hitch – a Clove Hitch is not recommended.

When finished, tie off the working end either below the loop using Half Hitches or better, at the anchor point, by making two or three wraps to take the strain before finishing with Half Hitches (see Step 1).

METHOD 1

STEP 1

Pass the rope over the load and, at a point within reach, make a fixed loop (a Farmer's Loop or Butterfly Loop is recommended). Now take the working end down and around a second anchor point on the opposite side to the first, and then back up and through the loop made at Step 1. Pull the working end down using the loop as a makeshift pulley but be careful – you can damage your load by pulling too hard. This method is safe and works well, but if the same loop in the rope is used repeatedly, wear will result, damaging the whole rope.

METHOD 2

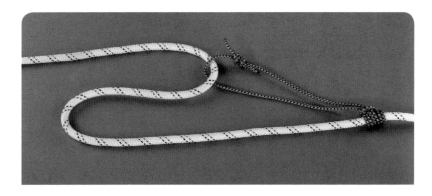

STEP 2　　Use a rope sling and Prusik Knot attached to the rope to form the loop. If this sling is damaged, only a short piece of rope is lost and this can easily be replaced. This works well for small loads, e.g. on a sack truck.

METHOD 3

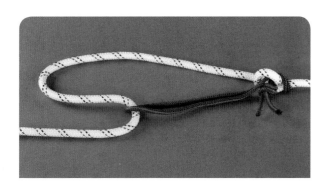

STEP 3

Start by making a short sling from a piece of rope (a sound short piece recovered from a damaged rope will be economical). The ends can be tied with a simple Overhand Knot as this sits well. In the main rope, make a loop as if starting a Bowline, but instead of taking the rope end up through the loop around the standing part and back down through the loop, use the sling so that the knotted part goes up, around and down – making it easily attached and easily removed and replaced but safe in use.

Uses　　The knot for roping down a load on a roof rack or trailer.

VERSATACKLE

Not a knot in itself but a way of applying tension to a rope either around an object (such as a large bundle) or stretched around two points, perhaps to hold a load in position. Once tied, the tackle is self-locking yet easily undone.

TO TIE

At one end of a rope, tie a loop knot, for example an Angler's Loop. Then tie a midline loop a distance down the rope – a Butterfly Knot or Farmer's Loop, for example. The distance between these knots needs to be slightly more than the distance between the attachment points or somewhat less than the diameter of a bundle.

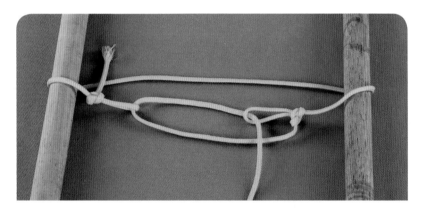

STEP 1   Place the rope around the two attachment points, with the loops on the same side and pass the end of the rope from the Butterfly Knot and through the end loop and then lead the end of the rope back through the Butterfly Loop.

Uses   Use this in a van or on a roof rack or trailer to hold a load in place. May be found easier to use than a Trucker's Hitch.

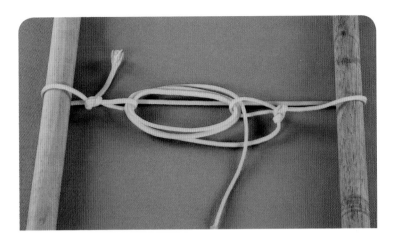

STEP 2 Continue to lead the end of the rope tightly through each loop in turn until at least three circuits have been made. Make sure that the coils between the loops tighten evenly.

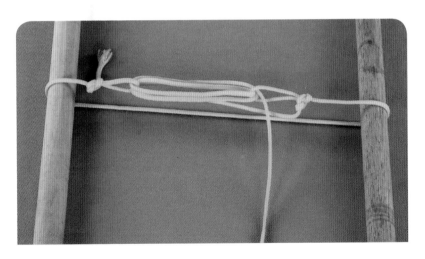

The end should now be locked and will not slip, but if leaving this in place for some time (or leaving it unattended), take the end around the coils and back under itself to form a Half Hitch, which is then pulled tight for extra security.

STEP 3

GLOSSARY

TERM	DEFINITION
Back-up knot	An extra knot added for security especially where failure would be especially dangerous
Bend	A knot for joining two (or more) ropes
Bight	A curve in a rope. If the curve is completely closed it becomes a loop – see Loop below
Braided rope	Rope made by interweaving strands rather than twisting three together as in laid rope
Bungee cord	Elastic cord made up of rubber strands or strips surrounded by a braided sheath
Cable-laid	Cable-laid rope is made from strands which themselves are made from three or more strands twisted together. It is more stable than hawser-laid rope
Cord	Technically, material less than 10 mm in diameter. See Rope
Eye	A small loop in a rope end
Follow round	To use cord to trace a path through a knot thus creating a second or third pass through the knot – used most often in decorative knots. For an example, see the Water Knot
Half Hitch	A simple knot made by passing the end of a rope around itself, another rope or an object and then through its own loop. The same structure as an Overhand Knot
Hawser-laid	Hawser-laid rope is made from three strands twisted together
Hitch	A knot for attaching a rope or cord to an object (e.g. a ring) or another rope where the two ropes are not

TERM	DEFINITION
	being tied together to form one (see Bend)
Kermantel	Rope consisting of an outer sheath (usually braided) and a central core (which may be braided or loose strands)
Knot security	A knot's resistance to slipping
Knot strength	The strength of cordage once it has been knotted – knots reduce the original strength of rope etc.
Laid rope	Rope formed from twisted strands (which may themselves be made from strands twisted in the opposite direction)
Lanyard	A cord made into a loop used to attach something around the neck, to a belt or to a uniform for example
Lay (of rope)	The direction in which the strands of the rope are twisted. To unlay a rope is to untwist the strands
Lead	The direction the working end of a rope takes
Loop	A rope which forms a circle, the ends of which are joined or at least cross over one another
MBS	Minimum Breaking Strength of rope – but see Safe Working Load
Noose	A loop which is not of fixed size, i.e. it can easily be adjusted. See Slip Knot
Prusik, to	Term used by climbers to indicate using a Prusik Knot on a sling used to ascend a rope
Rope	Technically, to be called rope, material must be at least 10 mm in diameter. In practice, the term is used loosely to describe any thick cordage from about 6 mm

TERM	DEFINITION
Round Turn	A complete turn of rope or cord around an object (or another rope) encircling it
Safe Working Load	Usually shown as 'SWL', this is the maximum load that should be placed on a rope. Set by the manufacturer, it allows for some wear and sub-optimal state of the rope in actual use – it is usually about 20 to 25 per cent of the actual breaking strain of new rope, but may be less. It is potentially dangerous to exceed it
Shackle	Horseshoe-shaped metal fitting attached to a chain or fitting such as an eye bolt. It has a removable pin
Shock cord	See Bungee cord
Sling	A circle of rope or tape either knotted at the ends or stitched (in the case of tape)
Slip Knot	A knot tied in the end of a cord using an Overhand Knot around the standing part. See also Noose
Slipped knot	Knot where the end of the knot has been tucked to enable the knot to be undone by pulling on the end
Standing end	The end of a rope or cord which is inactive during the formation of a knot
SWL	See Safe Working Load
Thimble	A metal or plastic fitting inserted into the eye in a rope. Usually heart-shaped but sometimes circular, it has a groove into which the rope fits and is therefore sold by reference to the thickness of the rope. Helps to stop wear on the rope
Tie-in knot	Knot used to attach a rope to a climber's harness
Working end	The end of the rope used to form a knot

ALTERNATIVE NAME	IN BOOK
Alpine Butterfly Loop	Butterfly Loop
Bale Sling Hitch	Cow Hitch
Bosun's Whistle Knot	Lanyard Knot
Common Bend	Sheet Bend
Diamond Knot, 2 strand	Lanyard Knot
Fisherman's Bend	Anchor Hitch
Grapevine Bend	Double/Triple Fisherman's Knot
Grinner Knot	Double Fisherman's Knot
Half Knot	Overhand Knot
Kalmyk Loop	Slipped Eskimo Bowline
Lanyard Hitch	Cow Hitch
Lark's Head	Cow Hitch
Magnus Hitch	Rolling Hitch
Midshipman's Hitch	Tautline Hitch
Oysterman's Stopper	Ashley's Stopper
Perfection Loop	Angler's Loop
Rigger's Bend	Hunter's Bend
Ring Hitch	Girth Hitch
Rosendahl Bend	Zeppelin Bend
Square Knot	Reef Knot
Strap Hitch	Girth Hitch
Tautline Hitch	Rolling Hitch
Thumb Knot	Overhand Knot or Loop

INDEX OF KNOTS

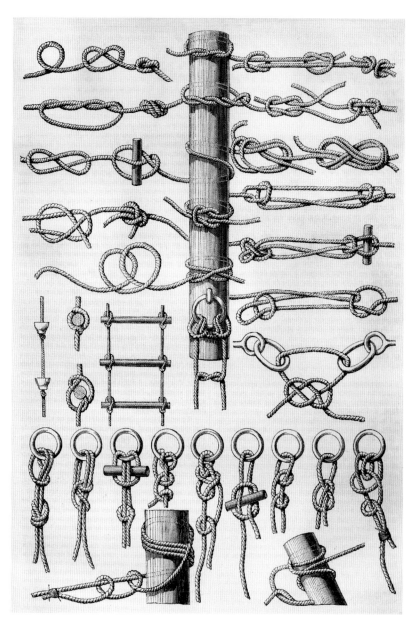

A table of knots published in Paris in 1845

Author Barry Mault is a prominent member of the International Guild of Knot Tyers (IGKT) and he is a moderator of their web forum as well as being Treasurer of the Waterways Craft Guild. His main interest is in practical knots, though he also works with parachute cord, making small decorative items.